Name

Address

Telephone Number

E-mail Address

Gift

Save The Day Card Sent	Invitation Sent	R.S.V.P Received	Thank You Sent	Number Attending

Name

Address

Telephone Number

E-mail Address

Gift

Save The Day Card Sent	Invitation Sent	R.S.V.P Received	Thank You Sent	Number Attending

Name

Address

Telephone Number

E-mail Address

Gift

Save The Day Card Sent	Invitation Sent	R.S.V.P Received	Thank You Sent	Number Attending

Name

Address

Telephone Number

E-mail Address

Gift

Save The Day Card Sent	Invitation Sent	R.S.V.P Received	Thank You Sent	Number Attending

Name

Address

Telephone Number

E-mail Address

Gift

Save The Day Card Sent	Invitation Sent	R.S.V.P Received	Thank You Sent	Number Attending

Guest List Planner

Name

Address

Telephone Number

E-mail Address

Gift

| Save The Day Card Sent | Invitation Sent | R.S.V.P Received | Thank You Sent | Number Attending |

Name

Address

Telephone Number

E-mail Address

Gift

| Save The Day Card Sent | Invitation Sent | R.S.V.P Received | Thank You Sent | Number Attending |

Name

Address

Telephone Number

E-mail Address

Gift

| Save The Day Card Sent | Invitation Sent | R.S.V.P Received | Thank You Sent | Number Attending |

Name

Address

Telephone Number

E-mail Address

Gift

| Save The Day Card Sent | Invitation Sent | R.S.V.P Received | Thank You Sent | Number Attending |

Name

Address

Telephone Number

E-mail Address

Gift

| Save The Day Card Sent | Invitation Sent | R.S.V.P Received | Thank You Sent | Number Attending |

Guest List Planner

Name

Address

Telephone Number

E-mail Address

Gift

| Save The Day Card Sent | Invitation Sent | R.S.V.P Received | Thank You Sent | Number Attending |

Name

Address

Telephone Number

E-mail Address

Gift

| Save The Day Card Sent | Invitation Sent | R.S.V.P Received | Thank You Sent | Number Attending |

Name

Address

Telephone Number

E-mail Address

Gift

| Save The Day Card Sent | Invitation Sent | R.S.V.P Received | Thank You Sent | Number Attending |

Name

Address

Telephone Number

E-mail Address

Gift

| Save The Day Card Sent | Invitation Sent | R.S.V.P Received | Thank You Sent | Number Attending |

Name

Address

Telephone Number

E-mail Address

Gift

| Save The Day Card Sent | Invitation Sent | R.S.V.P Received | Thank You Sent | Number Attending |

Guest List Planner

Name

Address

Telephone Number

E-mail Address

Gift

| Save The Day Card Sent | Invitation Sent | R.S.V.P Received | Thank You Sent | Number Attending |

Name

Address

Telephone Number

E-mail Address

Gift

| Save The Day Card Sent | Invitation Sent | R.S.V.P Received | Thank You Sent | Number Attending |

Name

Address

Telephone Number

E-mail Address

Gift

| Save The Day Card Sent | Invitation Sent | R.S.V.P Received | Thank You Sent | Number Attending |

Name

Address

Telephone Number

E-mail Address

Gift

| Save The Day Card Sent | Invitation Sent | R.S.V.P Received | Thank You Sent | Number Attending |

Name

Address

Telephone Number

E-mail Address

Gift

| Save The Day Card Sent | Invitation Sent | R.S.V.P Received | Thank You Sent | Number Attending |

Guest List Planner

Name

Address

Telephone Number

E-mail Address

Gift

| Save The Day Card Sent | Invitation Sent | R.S.V.P Received | Thank You Sent | Number Attending |

Name

Address

Telephone Number

E-mail Address

Gift

| Save The Day Card Sent | Invitation Sent | R.S.V.P Received | Thank You Sent | Number Attending |

Name

Address

Telephone Number

E-mail Address

Gift

| Save The Day Card Sent | Invitation Sent | R.S.V.P Received | Thank You Sent | Number Attending |

Name

Address

Telephone Number

E-mail Address

Gift

| Save The Day Card Sent | Invitation Sent | R.S.V.P Received | Thank You Sent | Number Attending |

Name

Address

Telephone Number

E-mail Address

Gift

| Save The Day Card Sent | Invitation Sent | R.S.V.P Received | Thank You Sent | Number Attending |

Guest List Planner

Name

Address

Telephone Number

E-mail Address

Gift

| Save The Day Card Sent | Invitation Sent | R.S.V.P Received | Thank You Sent | Number Attending |

Name

Address

Telephone Number

E-mail Address

Gift

| Save The Day Card Sent | Invitation Sent | R.S.V.P Received | Thank You Sent | Number Attending |

Name

Address

Telephone Number

E-mail Address

Gift

| Save The Day Card Sent | Invitation Sent | R.S.V.P Received | Thank You Sent | Number Attending |

Name

Address

Telephone Number

E-mail Address

Gift

| Save The Day Card Sent | Invitation Sent | R.S.V.P Received | Thank You Sent | Number Attending |

Name

Address

Telephone Number

E-mail Address

Gift

| Save The Day Card Sent | Invitation Sent | R.S.V.P Received | Thank You Sent | Number Attending |

Guest List Planner

Name

Address

Telephone Number

E-mail Address

Gift

| Save The Day Card Sent | Invitation Sent | R.S.V.P Received | Thank You Sent | Number Attending |

Name

Address

Telephone Number

E-mail Address

Gift

| Save The Day Card Sent | Invitation Sent | R.S.V.P Received | Thank You Sent | Number Attending |

Name

Address

Telephone Number

E-mail Address

Gift

| Save The Day Card Sent | Invitation Sent | R.S.V.P Received | Thank You Sent | Number Attending |

Name

Address

Telephone Number

E-mail Address

Gift

| Save The Day Card Sent | Invitation Sent | R.S.V.P Received | Thank You Sent | Number Attending |

Name

Address

Telephone Number

E-mail Address

Gift

| Save The Day Card Sent | Invitation Sent | R.S.V.P Received | Thank You Sent | Number Attending |

Guest List Planner

Name

Address

Telephone Number

E-mail Address

Gift

| Save The Day Card Sent | Invitation Sent | R.S.V.P Received | Thank You Sent | Number Attending |

Name

Address

Telephone Number

E-mail Address

Gift

| Save The Day Card Sent | Invitation Sent | R.S.V.P Received | Thank You Sent | Number Attending |

Name

Address

Telephone Number

E-mail Address

Gift

| Save The Day Card Sent | Invitation Sent | R.S.V.P Received | Thank You Sent | Number Attending |

Name

Address

Telephone Number

E-mail Address

Gift

| Save The Day Card Sent | Invitation Sent | R.S.V.P Received | Thank You Sent | Number Attending |

Name

Address

Telephone Number

E-mail Address

Gift

| Save The Day Card Sent | Invitation Sent | R.S.V.P Received | Thank You Sent | Number Attending |

Guest List Planner

Name

Address

Telephone Number

E-mail Address

Gift

| Save The Day Card Sent | Invitation Sent | R.S.V.P Received | Thank You Sent | Number Attending |

Name

Address

Telephone Number

E-mail Address

Gift

| Save The Day Card Sent | Invitation Sent | R.S.V.P Received | Thank You Sent | Number Attending |

Name

Address

Telephone Number

E-mail Address

Gift

| Save The Day Card Sent | Invitation Sent | R.S.V.P Received | Thank You Sent | Number Attending |

Name

Address

Telephone Number

E-mail Address

Gift

| Save The Day Card Sent | Invitation Sent | R.S.V.P Received | Thank You Sent | Number Attending |

Name

Address

Telephone Number

E-mail Address

Gift

| Save The Day Card Sent | Invitation Sent | R.S.V.P Received | Thank You Sent | Number Attending |

Guest List Planner

Name

Address

Telephone Number

E-mail Address

Gift

| Save The Day Card Sent | Invitation Sent | R.S.V.P Received | Thank You Sent | Number Attending |

Name

Address

Telephone Number

E-mail Address

Gift

| Save The Day Card Sent | Invitation Sent | R.S.V.P Received | Thank You Sent | Number Attending |

Name

Address

Telephone Number

E-mail Address

Gift

| Save The Day Card Sent | Invitation Sent | R.S.V.P Received | Thank You Sent | Number Attending |

Name

Address

Telephone Number

E-mail Address

Gift

| Save The Day Card Sent | Invitation Sent | R.S.V.P Received | Thank You Sent | Number Attending |

Name

Address

Telephone Number

E-mail Address

Gift

| Save The Day Card Sent | Invitation Sent | R.S.V.P Received | Thank You Sent | Number Attending |

Guest List Planner

Name

Address

Telephone Number

E-mail Address

Gift

Save The Day　　　　　Invitation　　　　　R.S.V.P　　　　　Thank You　　　　　Number
Card Sent　　　　　　　Sent　　　　　　　　Received　　　　　Sent　　　　　　　　Attending

Name

Address

Telephone Number

E-mail Address

Gift

Save The Day　　　　　Invitation　　　　　R.S.V.P　　　　　Thank You　　　　　Number
Card Sent　　　　　　　Sent　　　　　　　　Received　　　　　Sent　　　　　　　　Attending

Name

Address

Telephone Number

E-mail Address

Gift

Save The Day　　　　　Invitation　　　　　R.S.V.P　　　　　Thank You　　　　　Number
Card Sent　　　　　　　Sent　　　　　　　　Received　　　　　Sent　　　　　　　　Attending

Name

Address

Telephone Number

E-mail Address

Gift

Save The Day　　　　　Invitation　　　　　R.S.V.P　　　　　Thank You　　　　　Number
Card Sent　　　　　　　Sent　　　　　　　　Received　　　　　Sent　　　　　　　　Attending

Name

Address

Telephone Number

E-mail Address

Gift

Save The Day　　　　　Invitation　　　　　R.S.V.P　　　　　Thank You　　　　　Number
Card Sent　　　　　　　Sent　　　　　　　　Received　　　　　Sent　　　　　　　　Attending

Guest List Planner

Name

Address

Telephone Number

E-mail Address

Gift

| Save The Day Card Sent | Invitation Sent | R.S.V.P Received | Thank You Sent | Number Attending |

Name

Address

Telephone Number

E-mail Address

Gift

| Save The Day Card Sent | Invitation Sent | R.S.V.P Received | Thank You Sent | Number Attending |

Name

Address

Telephone Number

E-mail Address

Gift

| Save The Day Card Sent | Invitation Sent | R.S.V.P Received | Thank You Sent | Number Attending |

Name

Address

Telephone Number

E-mail Address

Gift

| Save The Day Card Sent | Invitation Sent | R.S.V.P Received | Thank You Sent | Number Attending |

Name

Address

Telephone Number

E-mail Address

Gift

| Save The Day Card Sent | Invitation Sent | R.S.V.P Received | Thank You Sent | Number Attending |

Guest List Planner

Name

Address

Telephone Number

E-mail Address

Gift

Save The Day Card Sent	Invitation Sent	R.S.V.P Received	Thank You Sent	Number Attending

Name

Address

Telephone Number

E-mail Address

Gift

Save The Day Card Sent	Invitation Sent	R.S.V.P Received	Thank You Sent	Number Attending

Name

Address

Telephone Number

E-mail Address

Gift

Save The Day Card Sent	Invitation Sent	R.S.V.P Received	Thank You Sent	Number Attending

Name

Address

Telephone Number

E-mail Address

Gift

Save The Day Card Sent	Invitation Sent	R.S.V.P Received	Thank You Sent	Number Attending

Name

Address

Telephone Number

E-mail Address

Gift

Save The Day Card Sent	Invitation Sent	R.S.V.P Received	Thank You Sent	Number Attending

Guest List Planner

Name

Address

Telephone Number

E-mail Address

Gift

| Save The Day Card Sent | Invitation Sent | R.S.V.P Received | Thank You Sent | Number Attending |

Name

Address

Telephone Number

E-mail Address

Gift

| Save The Day Card Sent | Invitation Sent | R.S.V.P Received | Thank You Sent | Number Attending |

Name

Address

Telephone Number

E-mail Address

Gift

| Save The Day Card Sent | Invitation Sent | R.S.V.P Received | Thank You Sent | Number Attending |

Name

Address

Telephone Number

E-mail Address

Gift

| Save The Day Card Sent | Invitation Sent | R.S.V.P Received | Thank You Sent | Number Attending |

Name

Address

Telephone Number

E-mail Address

Gift

| Save The Day Card Sent | Invitation Sent | R.S.V.P Received | Thank You Sent | Number Attending |

Guest List Planner

Name
Address
Telephone Number
E-mail Address
Gift

Save The Day Card Sent | Invitation Sent | R.S.V.P Received | Thank You Sent | Number Attending

Name
Address
Telephone Number
E-mail Address
Gift

Save The Day Card Sent | Invitation Sent | R.S.V.P Received | Thank You Sent | Number Attending

Name
Address
Telephone Number
E-mail Address
Gift

Save The Day Card Sent | Invitation Sent | R.S.V.P Received | Thank You Sent | Number Attending

Name
Address
Telephone Number
E-mail Address
Gift

Save The Day Card Sent | Invitation Sent | R.S.V.P Received | Thank You Sent | Number Attending

Name
Address
Telephone Number
E-mail Address
Gift

Save The Day Card Sent | Invitation Sent | R.S.V.P Received | Thank You Sent | Number Attending

Guest List Planner

Name
Address
Telephone Number
E-mail Address
Gift

Save The Day Card Sent	Invitation Sent	R.S.V.P Received	Thank You Sent	Number Attending

Name
Address
Telephone Number
E-mail Address
Gift

Save The Day Card Sent	Invitation Sent	R.S.V.P Received	Thank You Sent	Number Attending

Name
Address
Telephone Number
E-mail Address
Gift

Save The Day Card Sent	Invitation Sent	R.S.V.P Received	Thank You Sent	Number Attending

Name
Address
Telephone Number
E-mail Address
Gift

Save The Day Card Sent	Invitation Sent	R.S.V.P Received	Thank You Sent	Number Attending

Name
Address
Telephone Number
E-mail Address
Gift

Save The Day Card Sent	Invitation Sent	R.S.V.P Received	Thank You Sent	Number Attending

Guest List Planner

Name

Address

Telephone Number

E-mail Address

Gift

Save The Day Card Sent	Invitation Sent	R.S.V.P Received	Thank You Sent	Number Attending

Name

Address

Telephone Number

E-mail Address

Gift

Save The Day Card Sent	Invitation Sent	R.S.V.P Received	Thank You Sent	Number Attending

Name

Address

Telephone Number

E-mail Address

Gift

Save The Day Card Sent	Invitation Sent	R.S.V.P Received	Thank You Sent	Number Attending

Name

Address

Telephone Number

E-mail Address

Gift

Save The Day Card Sent	Invitation Sent	R.S.V.P Received	Thank You Sent	Number Attending

Name

Address

Telephone Number

E-mail Address

Gift

Save The Day Card Sent	Invitation Sent	R.S.V.P Received	Thank You Sent	Number Attending

Guest List Planner

Name

Address

Telephone Number

E-mail Address

Gift

| Save The Day Card Sent | Invitation Sent | R.S.V.P Received | Thank You Sent | Number Attending |

Name

Address

Telephone Number

E-mail Address

Gift

| Save The Day Card Sent | Invitation Sent | R.S.V.P Received | Thank You Sent | Number Attending |

Name

Address

Telephone Number

E-mail Address

Gift

| Save The Day Card Sent | Invitation Sent | R.S.V.P Received | Thank You Sent | Number Attending |

Name

Address

Telephone Number

E-mail Address

Gift

| Save The Day Card Sent | Invitation Sent | R.S.V.P Received | Thank You Sent | Number Attending |

Name

Address

Telephone Number

E-mail Address

Gift

| Save The Day Card Sent | Invitation Sent | R.S.V.P Received | Thank You Sent | Number Attending |

Guest List Planner

Name

Address

Telephone Number

E-mail Address

Gift

| Save The Day Card Sent | Invitation Sent | R.S.V.P Received | Thank You Sent | Number Attending |

Name

Address

Telephone Number

E-mail Address

Gift

| Save The Day Card Sent | Invitation Sent | R.S.V.P Received | Thank You Sent | Number Attending |

Name

Address

Telephone Number

E-mail Address

Gift

| Save The Day Card Sent | Invitation Sent | R.S.V.P Received | Thank You Sent | Number Attending |

Name

Address

Telephone Number

E-mail Address

Gift

| Save The Day Card Sent | Invitation Sent | R.S.V.P Received | Thank You Sent | Number Attending |

Name

Address

Telephone Number

E-mail Address

Gift

| Save The Day Card Sent | Invitation Sent | R.S.V.P Received | Thank You Sent | Number Attending |

Guest List Planner

Name

Address

Telephone Number

E-mail Address

Gift

Save The Day Card Sent	Invitation Sent	R.S.V.P Received	Thank You Sent	Number Attending

Name

Address

Telephone Number

E-mail Address

Gift

Save The Day Card Sent	Invitation Sent	R.S.V.P Received	Thank You Sent	Number Attending

Name

Address

Telephone Number

E-mail Address

Gift

Save The Day Card Sent	Invitation Sent	R.S.V.P Received	Thank You Sent	Number Attending

Name

Address

Telephone Number

E-mail Address

Gift

Save The Day Card Sent	Invitation Sent	R.S.V.P Received	Thank You Sent	Number Attending

Name

Address

Telephone Number

E-mail Address

Gift

Save The Day Card Sent	Invitation Sent	R.S.V.P Received	Thank You Sent	Number Attending

Guest List Planner

Name

Address

Telephone Number

E-mail Address

Gift

Save The Day Card Sent	Invitation Sent	R.S.V.P Received	Thank You Sent	Number Attending

Name

Address

Telephone Number

E-mail Address

Gift

Save The Day Card Sent	Invitation Sent	R.S.V.P Received	Thank You Sent	Number Attending

Name

Address

Telephone Number

E-mail Address

Gift

Save The Day Card Sent	Invitation Sent	R.S.V.P Received	Thank You Sent	Number Attending

Name

Address

Telephone Number

E-mail Address

Gift

Save The Day Card Sent	Invitation Sent	R.S.V.P Received	Thank You Sent	Number Attending

Name

Address

Telephone Number

E-mail Address

Gift

Save The Day Card Sent	Invitation Sent	R.S.V.P Received	Thank You Sent	Number Attending

Guest List Planner

Name

Address

Telephone Number

E-mail Address

Gift

| Save The Day Card Sent | Invitation Sent | R.S.V.P Received | Thank You Sent | Number Attending |

Name

Address

Telephone Number

E-mail Address

Gift

| Save The Day Card Sent | Invitation Sent | R.S.V.P Received | Thank You Sent | Number Attending |

Name

Address

Telephone Number

E-mail Address

Gift

| Save The Day Card Sent | Invitation Sent | R.S.V.P Received | Thank You Sent | Number Attending |

Name

Address

Telephone Number

E-mail Address

Gift

| Save The Day Card Sent | Invitation Sent | R.S.V.P Received | Thank You Sent | Number Attending |

Name

Address

Telephone Number

E-mail Address

Gift

| Save The Day Card Sent | Invitation Sent | R.S.V.P Received | Thank You Sent | Number Attending |

Guest List Planner

Name

Address

Telephone Number

E-mail Address

Gift

Save The Day Card Sent   Invitation Sent   R.S.V.P Received   Thank You Sent   Number Attending

Name

Address

Telephone Number

E-mail Address

Gift

Save The Day Card Sent   Invitation Sent   R.S.V.P Received   Thank You Sent   Number Attending

Name

Address

Telephone Number

E-mail Address

Gift

Save The Day Card Sent   Invitation Sent   R.S.V.P Received   Thank You Sent   Number Attending

Name

Address

Telephone Number

E-mail Address

Gift

Save The Day Card Sent   Invitation Sent   R.S.V.P Received   Thank You Sent   Number Attending

Name

Address

Telephone Number

E-mail Address

Gift

Save The Day Card Sent   Invitation Sent   R.S.V.P Received   Thank You Sent   Number Attending

Guest List Planner

Name

Address

Telephone Number

E-mail Address

Gift

Save The Day Card Sent	Invitation Sent	R.S.V.P Received	Thank You Sent	Number Attending

Name

Address

Telephone Number

E-mail Address

Gift

Save The Day Card Sent	Invitation Sent	R.S.V.P Received	Thank You Sent	Number Attending

Name

Address

Telephone Number

E-mail Address

Gift

Save The Day Card Sent	Invitation Sent	R.S.V.P Received	Thank You Sent	Number Attending

Name

Address

Telephone Number

E-mail Address

Gift

Save The Day Card Sent	Invitation Sent	R.S.V.P Received	Thank You Sent	Number Attending

Name

Address

Telephone Number

E-mail Address

Gift

Save The Day Card Sent	Invitation Sent	R.S.V.P Received	Thank You Sent	Number Attending

Guest List Planner

Name

Address

Telephone Number

E-mail Address

Gift

Save The Day Card Sent	Invitation Sent	R.S.V.P Received	Thank You Sent	Number Attending

Name

Address

Telephone Number

E-mail Address

Gift

Save The Day Card Sent	Invitation Sent	R.S.V.P Received	Thank You Sent	Number Attending

Name

Address

Telephone Number

E-mail Address

Gift

Save The Day Card Sent	Invitation Sent	R.S.V.P Received	Thank You Sent	Number Attending

Name

Address

Telephone Number

E-mail Address

Gift

Save The Day Card Sent	Invitation Sent	R.S.V.P Received	Thank You Sent	Number Attending

Name

Address

Telephone Number

E-mail Address

Gift

Save The Day Card Sent	Invitation Sent	R.S.V.P Received	Thank You Sent	Number Attending

Guest List Planner

Name
Address
Telephone Number
E-mail Address
Gift

Save The Day Card Sent   Invitation Sent   R.S.V.P Received   Thank You Sent   Number Attending

Name
Address
Telephone Number
E-mail Address
Gift

Save The Day Card Sent   Invitation Sent   R.S.V.P Received   Thank You Sent   Number Attending

Name
Address
Telephone Number
E-mail Address
Gift

Save The Day Card Sent   Invitation Sent   R.S.V.P Received   Thank You Sent   Number Attending

Name
Address
Telephone Number
E-mail Address
Gift

Save The Day Card Sent   Invitation Sent   R.S.V.P Received   Thank You Sent   Number Attending

Name
Address
Telephone Number
E-mail Address
Gift

Save The Day Card Sent   Invitation Sent   R.S.V.P Received   Thank You Sent   Number Attending

Guest List Planner

Name
Address
Telephone Number
E-mail Address
Gift

Save The Day Card Sent | Invitation Sent | R.S.V.P Received | Thank You Sent | Number Attending

Name
Address
Telephone Number
E-mail Address
Gift

Save The Day Card Sent | Invitation Sent | R.S.V.P Received | Thank You Sent | Number Attending

Name
Address
Telephone Number
E-mail Address
Gift

Save The Day Card Sent | Invitation Sent | R.S.V.P Received | Thank You Sent | Number Attending

Name
Address
Telephone Number
E-mail Address
Gift

Save The Day Card Sent | Invitation Sent | R.S.V.P Received | Thank You Sent | Number Attending

Name
Address
Telephone Number
E-mail Address
Gift

Save The Day Card Sent | Invitation Sent | R.S.V.P Received | Thank You Sent | Number Attending

Guest List Planner

Name
Address
Telephone Number
E-mail Address
Gift

Save The Day Card Sent | Invitation Sent | R.S.V.P Received | Thank You Sent | Number Attending

Name
Address
Telephone Number
E-mail Address
Gift

Save The Day Card Sent | Invitation Sent | R.S.V.P Received | Thank You Sent | Number Attending

Name
Address
Telephone Number
E-mail Address
Gift

Save The Day Card Sent | Invitation Sent | R.S.V.P Received | Thank You Sent | Number Attending

Name
Address
Telephone Number
E-mail Address
Gift

Save The Day Card Sent | Invitation Sent | R.S.V.P Received | Thank You Sent | Number Attending

Name
Address
Telephone Number
E-mail Address
Gift

Save The Day Card Sent | Invitation Sent | R.S.V.P Received | Thank You Sent | Number Attending

Guest List Planner

Name

Address

Telephone Number

E-mail Address

Gift

| Save The Day Card Sent | Invitation Sent | R.S.V.P Received | Thank You Sent | Number Attending |

Name

Address

Telephone Number

E-mail Address

Gift

| Save The Day Card Sent | Invitation Sent | R.S.V.P Received | Thank You Sent | Number Attending |

Name

Address

Telephone Number

E-mail Address

Gift

| Save The Day Card Sent | Invitation Sent | R.S.V.P Received | Thank You Sent | Number Attending |

Name

Address

Telephone Number

E-mail Address

Gift

| Save The Day Card Sent | Invitation Sent | R.S.V.P Received | Thank You Sent | Number Attending |

Name

Address

Telephone Number

E-mail Address

Gift

| Save The Day Card Sent | Invitation Sent | R.S.V.P Received | Thank You Sent | Number Attending |

Guest List Planner

Name

Address

Telephone Number

E-mail Address

Gift

| Save The Day Card Sent | Invitation Sent | R.S.V.P Received | Thank You Sent | Number Attending |

Name

Address

Telephone Number

E-mail Address

Gift

| Save The Day Card Sent | Invitation Sent | R.S.V.P Received | Thank You Sent | Number Attending |

Name

Address

Telephone Number

E-mail Address

Gift

| Save The Day Card Sent | Invitation Sent | R.S.V.P Received | Thank You Sent | Number Attending |

Name

Address

Telephone Number

E-mail Address

Gift

| Save The Day Card Sent | Invitation Sent | R.S.V.P Received | Thank You Sent | Number Attending |

Name

Address

Telephone Number

E-mail Address

Gift

| Save The Day Card Sent | Invitation Sent | R.S.V.P Received | Thank You Sent | Number Attending |

Guest List Planner

Name

Address

Telephone Number

E-mail Address

Gift

| Save The Day Card Sent | Invitation Sent | R.S.V.P Received | Thank You Sent | Number Attending |

Name

Address

Telephone Number

E-mail Address

Gift

| Save The Day Card Sent | Invitation Sent | R.S.V.P Received | Thank You Sent | Number Attending |

Name

Address

Telephone Number

E-mail Address

Gift

| Save The Day Card Sent | Invitation Sent | R.S.V.P Received | Thank You Sent | Number Attending |

Name

Address

Telephone Number

E-mail Address

Gift

| Save The Day Card Sent | Invitation Sent | R.S.V.P Received | Thank You Sent | Number Attending |

Name

Address

Telephone Number

E-mail Address

Gift

| Save The Day Card Sent | Invitation Sent | R.S.V.P Received | Thank You Sent | Number Attending |

Guest List Planner

Name

Address

Telephone Number

E-mail Address

Gift

Save The Day Card Sent   Invitation Sent   R.S.V.P Received   Thank You Sent   Number Attending

Name

Address

Telephone Number

E-mail Address

Gift

Save The Day Card Sent   Invitation Sent   R.S.V.P Received   Thank You Sent   Number Attending

Name

Address

Telephone Number

E-mail Address

Gift

Save The Day Card Sent   Invitation Sent   R.S.V.P Received   Thank You Sent   Number Attending

Name

Address

Telephone Number

E-mail Address

Gift

Save The Day Card Sent   Invitation Sent   R.S.V.P Received   Thank You Sent   Number Attending

Name

Address

Telephone Number

E-mail Address

Gift

Save The Day Card Sent   Invitation Sent   R.S.V.P Received   Thank You Sent   Number Attending

Guest List Planner

Name
Address
Telephone Number
E-mail Address
Gift

Save The Day Invitation R.S.V.P Thank You Number
Card Sent Sent Received Sent Attending

Name
Address
Telephone Number
E-mail Address
Gift

Save The Day Invitation R.S.V.P Thank You Number
Card Sent Sent Received Sent Attending

Name
Address
Telephone Number
E-mail Address
Gift

Save The Day Invitation R.S.V.P Thank You Number
Card Sent Sent Received Sent Attending

Name
Address
Telephone Number
E-mail Address
Gift

Save The Day Invitation R.S.V.P Thank You Number
Card Sent Sent Received Sent Attending

Name
Address
Telephone Number
E-mail Address
Gift

Save The Day Invitation R.S.V.P Thank You Number
Card Sent Sent Received Sent Attending

Guest List Planner

Name

Address

Telephone Number

E-mail Address

Gift

| Save The Day Card Sent | Invitation Sent | R.S.V.P Received | Thank You Sent | Number Attending |

Name

Address

Telephone Number

E-mail Address

Gift

| Save The Day Card Sent | Invitation Sent | R.S.V.P Received | Thank You Sent | Number Attending |

Name

Address

Telephone Number

E-mail Address

Gift

| Save The Day Card Sent | Invitation Sent | R.S.V.P Received | Thank You Sent | Number Attending |

Name

Address

Telephone Number

E-mail Address

Gift

| Save The Day Card Sent | Invitation Sent | R.S.V.P Received | Thank You Sent | Number Attending |

Name

Address

Telephone Number

E-mail Address

Gift

| Save The Day Card Sent | Invitation Sent | R.S.V.P Received | Thank You Sent | Number Attending |

Guest List Planner

Name

Address

Telephone Number

E-mail Address

Gift

Save The Day Card Sent	Invitation Sent	R.S.V.P Received	Thank You Sent	Number Attending

Name

Address

Telephone Number

E-mail Address

Gift

Save The Day Card Sent	Invitation Sent	R.S.V.P Received	Thank You Sent	Number Attending

Name

Address

Telephone Number

E-mail Address

Gift

Save The Day Card Sent	Invitation Sent	R.S.V.P Received	Thank You Sent	Number Attending

Name

Address

Telephone Number

E-mail Address

Gift

Save The Day Card Sent	Invitation Sent	R.S.V.P Received	Thank You Sent	Number Attending

Name

Address

Telephone Number

E-mail Address

Gift

Save The Day Card Sent	Invitation Sent	R.S.V.P Received	Thank You Sent	Number Attending

Guest List Planner

Name

Address

Telephone Number

E-mail Address

Gift

Save The Day Card Sent	Invitation Sent	R.S.V.P Received	Thank You Sent	Number Attending

Name

Address

Telephone Number

E-mail Address

Gift

Save The Day Card Sent	Invitation Sent	R.S.V.P Received	Thank You Sent	Number Attending

Name

Address

Telephone Number

E-mail Address

Gift

Save The Day Card Sent	Invitation Sent	R.S.V.P Received	Thank You Sent	Number Attending

Name

Address

Telephone Number

E-mail Address

Gift

Save The Day Card Sent	Invitation Sent	R.S.V.P Received	Thank You Sent	Number Attending

Name

Address

Telephone Number

E-mail Address

Gift

Save The Day Card Sent	Invitation Sent	R.S.V.P Received	Thank You Sent	Number Attending

Guest List Planner

Name
Address
Telephone Number
E-mail Address
Gift

Save The Day Card Sent	Invitation Sent	R.S.V.P Received	Thank You Sent	Number Attending

Name
Address
Telephone Number
E-mail Address
Gift

Save The Day Card Sent	Invitation Sent	R.S.V.P Received	Thank You Sent	Number Attending

Name
Address
Telephone Number
E-mail Address
Gift

Save The Day Card Sent	Invitation Sent	R.S.V.P Received	Thank You Sent	Number Attending

Name
Address
Telephone Number
E-mail Address
Gift

Save The Day Card Sent	Invitation Sent	R.S.V.P Received	Thank You Sent	Number Attending

Name
Address
Telephone Number
E-mail Address
Gift

Save The Day Card Sent	Invitation Sent	R.S.V.P Received	Thank You Sent	Number Attending

Guest List Planner

Name

Address

Telephone Number

E-mail Address

Gift

| Save The Day Card Sent | Invitation Sent | R.S.V.P Received | Thank You Sent | Number Attending |

Name

Address

Telephone Number

E-mail Address

Gift

| Save The Day Card Sent | Invitation Sent | R.S.V.P Received | Thank You Sent | Number Attending |

Name

Address

Telephone Number

E-mail Address

Gift

| Save The Day Card Sent | Invitation Sent | R.S.V.P Received | Thank You Sent | Number Attending |

Name

Address

Telephone Number

E-mail Address

Gift

| Save The Day Card Sent | Invitation Sent | R.S.V.P Received | Thank You Sent | Number Attending |

Name

Address

Telephone Number

E-mail Address

Gift

| Save The Day Card Sent | Invitation Sent | R.S.V.P Received | Thank You Sent | Number Attending |

Guest List Planner

Name

Address

Telephone Number

E-mail Address

Gift

| Save The Day Card Sent | Invitation Sent | R.S.V.P Received | Thank You Sent | Number Attending |

Name

Address

Telephone Number

E-mail Address

Gift

| Save The Day Card Sent | Invitation Sent | R.S.V.P Received | Thank You Sent | Number Attending |

Name

Address

Telephone Number

E-mail Address

Gift

| Save The Day Card Sent | Invitation Sent | R.S.V.P Received | Thank You Sent | Number Attending |

Name

Address

Telephone Number

E-mail Address

Gift

| Save The Day Card Sent | Invitation Sent | R.S.V.P Received | Thank You Sent | Number Attending |

Name

Address

Telephone Number

E-mail Address

Gift

| Save The Day Card Sent | Invitation Sent | R.S.V.P Received | Thank You Sent | Number Attending |

Guest List Planner

Name

Address

Telephone Number

E-mail Address

Gift

| Save The Day Card Sent | Invitation Sent | R.S.V.P Received | Thank You Sent | Number Attending |

Name

Address

Telephone Number

E-mail Address

Gift

| Save The Day Card Sent | Invitation Sent | R.S.V.P Received | Thank You Sent | Number Attending |

Name

Address

Telephone Number

E-mail Address

Gift

| Save The Day Card Sent | Invitation Sent | R.S.V.P Received | Thank You Sent | Number Attending |

Name

Address

Telephone Number

E-mail Address

Gift

| Save The Day Card Sent | Invitation Sent | R.S.V.P Received | Thank You Sent | Number Attending |

Name

Address

Telephone Number

E-mail Address

Gift

| Save The Day Card Sent | Invitation Sent | R.S.V.P Received | Thank You Sent | Number Attending |

Guest List Planner

Name

Address

Telephone Number

E-mail Address

Gift

Save The Day Card Sent	Invitation Sent	R.S.V.P Received	Thank You Sent	Number Attending

Name

Address

Telephone Number

E-mail Address

Gift

Save The Day Card Sent	Invitation Sent	R.S.V.P Received	Thank You Sent	Number Attending

Name

Address

Telephone Number

E-mail Address

Gift

Save The Day Card Sent	Invitation Sent	R.S.V.P Received	Thank You Sent	Number Attending

Name

Address

Telephone Number

E-mail Address

Gift

Save The Day Card Sent	Invitation Sent	R.S.V.P Received	Thank You Sent	Number Attending

Name

Address

Telephone Number

E-mail Address

Gift

Save The Day Card Sent	Invitation Sent	R.S.V.P Received	Thank You Sent	Number Attending

Guest List Planner

Name

Address

Telephone Number

E-mail Address

Gift

Save The Day Card Sent	Invitation Sent	R.S.V.P Received	Thank You Sent	Number Attending

Name

Address

Telephone Number

E-mail Address

Gift

Save The Day Card Sent	Invitation Sent	R.S.V.P Received	Thank You Sent	Number Attending

Name

Address

Telephone Number

E-mail Address

Gift

Save The Day Card Sent	Invitation Sent	R.S.V.P Received	Thank You Sent	Number Attending

Name

Address

Telephone Number

E-mail Address

Gift

Save The Day Card Sent	Invitation Sent	R.S.V.P Received	Thank You Sent	Number Attending

Name

Address

Telephone Number

E-mail Address

Gift

Save The Day Card Sent	Invitation Sent	R.S.V.P Received	Thank You Sent	Number Attending

Guest List Planner

Name

Address

Telephone Number

E-mail Address

Gift

| Save The Day Card Sent | Invitation Sent | R.S.V.P Received | Thank You Sent | Number Attending |

Name

Address

Telephone Number

E-mail Address

Gift

| Save The Day Card Sent | Invitation Sent | R.S.V.P Received | Thank You Sent | Number Attending |

Name

Address

Telephone Number

E-mail Address

Gift

| Save The Day Card Sent | Invitation Sent | R.S.V.P Received | Thank You Sent | Number Attending |

Name

Address

Telephone Number

E-mail Address

Gift

| Save The Day Card Sent | Invitation Sent | R.S.V.P Received | Thank You Sent | Number Attending |

Name

Address

Telephone Number

E-mail Address

Gift

| Save The Day Card Sent | Invitation Sent | R.S.V.P Received | Thank You Sent | Number Attending |

Guest List Planner

Name

Address

Telephone Number

E-mail Address

Gift

| Save The Day Card Sent | Invitation Sent | R.S.V.P Received | Thank You Sent | Number Attending |

Name

Address

Telephone Number

E-mail Address

Gift

| Save The Day Card Sent | Invitation Sent | R.S.V.P Received | Thank You Sent | Number Attending |

Name

Address

Telephone Number

E-mail Address

Gift

| Save The Day Card Sent | Invitation Sent | R.S.V.P Received | Thank You Sent | Number Attending |

Name

Address

Telephone Number

E-mail Address

Gift

| Save The Day Card Sent | Invitation Sent | R.S.V.P Received | Thank You Sent | Number Attending |

Name

Address

Telephone Number

E-mail Address

Gift

| Save The Day Card Sent | Invitation Sent | R.S.V.P Received | Thank You Sent | Number Attending |

Guest List Planner

Name

Address

Telephone Number

E-mail Address

Gift

Save The Day Card Sent	Invitation Sent	R.S.V.P Received	Thank You Sent	Number Attending

Name

Address

Telephone Number

E-mail Address

Gift

Save The Day Card Sent	Invitation Sent	R.S.V.P Received	Thank You Sent	Number Attending

Name

Address

Telephone Number

E-mail Address

Gift

Save The Day Card Sent	Invitation Sent	R.S.V.P Received	Thank You Sent	Number Attending

Name

Address

Telephone Number

E-mail Address

Gift

Save The Day Card Sent	Invitation Sent	R.S.V.P Received	Thank You Sent	Number Attending

Name

Address

Telephone Number

E-mail Address

Gift

Save The Day Card Sent	Invitation Sent	R.S.V.P Received	Thank You Sent	Number Attending

Guest List Planner

Name
Address
Telephone Number
E-mail Address
Gift

Save The Day Card Sent	Invitation Sent	R.S.V.P Received	Thank You Sent	Number Attending

Name
Address
Telephone Number
E-mail Address
Gift

Save The Day Card Sent	Invitation Sent	R.S.V.P Received	Thank You Sent	Number Attending

Name
Address
Telephone Number
E-mail Address
Gift

Save The Day Card Sent	Invitation Sent	R.S.V.P Received	Thank You Sent	Number Attending

Name
Address
Telephone Number
E-mail Address
Gift

Save The Day Card Sent	Invitation Sent	R.S.V.P Received	Thank You Sent	Number Attending

Name
Address
Telephone Number
E-mail Address
Gift

Save The Day Card Sent	Invitation Sent	R.S.V.P Received	Thank You Sent	Number Attending

Guest List Planner

Name

Address

Telephone Number

E-mail Address

Gift

| Save The Day Card Sent | Invitation Sent | R.S.V.P Received | Thank You Sent | Number Attending |

Name

Address

Telephone Number

E-mail Address

Gift

| Save The Day Card Sent | Invitation Sent | R.S.V.P Received | Thank You Sent | Number Attending |

Name

Address

Telephone Number

E-mail Address

Gift

| Save The Day Card Sent | Invitation Sent | R.S.V.P Received | Thank You Sent | Number Attending |

Name

Address

Telephone Number

E-mail Address

Gift

| Save The Day Card Sent | Invitation Sent | R.S.V.P Received | Thank You Sent | Number Attending |

Name

Address

Telephone Number

E-mail Address

Gift

| Save The Day Card Sent | Invitation Sent | R.S.V.P Received | Thank You Sent | Number Attending |

Guest List Planner

Name

Address

Telephone Number

E-mail Address

Gift

Save The Day Card Sent   Invitation Sent   R.S.V.P Received   Thank You Sent   Number Attending

Name

Address

Telephone Number

E-mail Address

Gift

Save The Day Card Sent   Invitation Sent   R.S.V.P Received   Thank You Sent   Number Attending

Name

Address

Telephone Number

E-mail Address

Gift

Save The Day Card Sent   Invitation Sent   R.S.V.P Received   Thank You Sent   Number Attending

Name

Address

Telephone Number

E-mail Address

Gift

Save The Day Card Sent   Invitation Sent   R.S.V.P Received   Thank You Sent   Number Attending

Name

Address

Telephone Number

E-mail Address

Gift

Save The Day Card Sent   Invitation Sent   R.S.V.P Received   Thank You Sent   Number Attending

Guest List Planner

Name

Address

Telephone Number

E-mail Address

Gift

| Save The Day Card Sent | Invitation Sent | R.S.V.P Received | Thank You Sent | Number Attending |

Name

Address

Telephone Number

E-mail Address

Gift

| Save The Day Card Sent | Invitation Sent | R.S.V.P Received | Thank You Sent | Number Attending |

Name

Address

Telephone Number

E-mail Address

Gift

| Save The Day Card Sent | Invitation Sent | R.S.V.P Received | Thank You Sent | Number Attending |

Name

Address

Telephone Number

E-mail Address

Gift

| Save The Day Card Sent | Invitation Sent | R.S.V.P Received | Thank You Sent | Number Attending |

Name

Address

Telephone Number

E-mail Address

Gift

| Save The Day Card Sent | Invitation Sent | R.S.V.P Received | Thank You Sent | Number Attending |

Guest List Planner

Name

Address

Telephone Number

E-mail Address

Gift

| Save The Day Card Sent | Invitation Sent | R.S.V.P Received | Thank You Sent | Number Attending |

Name

Address

Telephone Number

E-mail Address

Gift

| Save The Day Card Sent | Invitation Sent | R.S.V.P Received | Thank You Sent | Number Attending |

Name

Address

Telephone Number

E-mail Address

Gift

| Save The Day Card Sent | Invitation Sent | R.S.V.P Received | Thank You Sent | Number Attending |

Name

Address

Telephone Number

E-mail Address

Gift

| Save The Day Card Sent | Invitation Sent | R.S.V.P Received | Thank You Sent | Number Attending |

Name

Address

Telephone Number

E-mail Address

Gift

| Save The Day Card Sent | Invitation Sent | R.S.V.P Received | Thank You Sent | Number Attending |

Guest List Planner

Name

Address

Telephone Number

E-mail Address

Gift

| Save The Day Card Sent | Invitation Sent | R.S.V.P Received | Thank You Sent | Number Attending |

Name

Address

Telephone Number

E-mail Address

Gift

| Save The Day Card Sent | Invitation Sent | R.S.V.P Received | Thank You Sent | Number Attending |

Name

Address

Telephone Number

E-mail Address

Gift

| Save The Day Card Sent | Invitation Sent | R.S.V.P Received | Thank You Sent | Number Attending |

Name

Address

Telephone Number

E-mail Address

Gift

| Save The Day Card Sent | Invitation Sent | R.S.V.P Received | Thank You Sent | Number Attending |

Name

Address

Telephone Number

E-mail Address

Gift

| Save The Day Card Sent | Invitation Sent | R.S.V.P Received | Thank You Sent | Number Attending |

Guest List Planner

Name

Address

Telephone Number

E-mail Address

Gift

Save The Day Card Sent | Invitation Sent | R.S.V.P Received | Thank You Sent | Number Attending

Name

Address

Telephone Number

E-mail Address

Gift

Save The Day Card Sent | Invitation Sent | R.S.V.P Received | Thank You Sent | Number Attending

Name

Address

Telephone Number

E-mail Address

Gift

Save The Day Card Sent | Invitation Sent | R.S.V.P Received | Thank You Sent | Number Attending

Name

Address

Telephone Number

E-mail Address

Gift

Save The Day Card Sent | Invitation Sent | R.S.V.P Received | Thank You Sent | Number Attending

Name

Address

Telephone Number

E-mail Address

Gift

Save The Day Card Sent | Invitation Sent | R.S.V.P Received | Thank You Sent | Number Attending

Guest List Planner

Name

Address

Telephone Number

E-mail Address

Gift

| Save The Day Card Sent | Invitation Sent | R.S.V.P Received | Thank You Sent | Number Attending |

Name

Address

Telephone Number

E-mail Address

Gift

| Save The Day Card Sent | Invitation Sent | R.S.V.P Received | Thank You Sent | Number Attending |

Name

Address

Telephone Number

E-mail Address

Gift

| Save The Day Card Sent | Invitation Sent | R.S.V.P Received | Thank You Sent | Number Attending |

Name

Address

Telephone Number

E-mail Address

Gift

| Save The Day Card Sent | Invitation Sent | R.S.V.P Received | Thank You Sent | Number Attending |

Name

Address

Telephone Number

E-mail Address

Gift

| Save The Day Card Sent | Invitation Sent | R.S.V.P Received | Thank You Sent | Number Attending |

Guest List Planner

Name

Address

Telephone Number

E-mail Address

Gift

Save The Day Card Sent	Invitation Sent	R.S.V.P Received	Thank You Sent	Number Attending

Name

Address

Telephone Number

E-mail Address

Gift

Save The Day Card Sent	Invitation Sent	R.S.V.P Received	Thank You Sent	Number Attending

Name

Address

Telephone Number

E-mail Address

Gift

Save The Day Card Sent	Invitation Sent	R.S.V.P Received	Thank You Sent	Number Attending

Name

Address

Telephone Number

E-mail Address

Gift

Save The Day Card Sent	Invitation Sent	R.S.V.P Received	Thank You Sent	Number Attending

Name

Address

Telephone Number

E-mail Address

Gift

Save The Day Card Sent	Invitation Sent	R.S.V.P Received	Thank You Sent	Number Attending

Guest List Planner

Name

Address

Telephone Number

E-mail Address

Gift

| Save The Day Card Sent | Invitation Sent | R.S.V.P Received | Thank You Sent | Number Attending |

Name

Address

Telephone Number

E-mail Address

Gift

| Save The Day Card Sent | Invitation Sent | R.S.V.P Received | Thank You Sent | Number Attending |

Name

Address

Telephone Number

E-mail Address

Gift

| Save The Day Card Sent | Invitation Sent | R.S.V.P Received | Thank You Sent | Number Attending |

Name

Address

Telephone Number

E-mail Address

Gift

| Save The Day Card Sent | Invitation Sent | R.S.V.P Received | Thank You Sent | Number Attending |

Name

Address

Telephone Number

E-mail Address

Gift

| Save The Day Card Sent | Invitation Sent | R.S.V.P Received | Thank You Sent | Number Attending |

Guest List Planner

Name

Address

Telephone Number

E-mail Address

Gift

Save The Day Card Sent	Invitation Sent	R.S.V.P Received	Thank You Sent	Number Attending

Name

Address

Telephone Number

E-mail Address

Gift

Save The Day Card Sent	Invitation Sent	R.S.V.P Received	Thank You Sent	Number Attending

Name

Address

Telephone Number

E-mail Address

Gift

Save The Day Card Sent	Invitation Sent	R.S.V.P Received	Thank You Sent	Number Attending

Name

Address

Telephone Number

E-mail Address

Gift

Save The Day Card Sent	Invitation Sent	R.S.V.P Received	Thank You Sent	Number Attending

Name

Address

Telephone Number

E-mail Address

Gift

Save The Day Card Sent	Invitation Sent	R.S.V.P Received	Thank You Sent	Number Attending

Guest List Planner

Name
Address
Telephone Number
E-mail Address
Gift

Save The Day Card Sent | Invitation Sent | R.S.V.P Received | Thank You Sent | Number Attending

---

Name
Address
Telephone Number
E-mail Address
Gift

Save The Day Card Sent | Invitation Sent | R.S.V.P Received | Thank You Sent | Number Attending

---

Name
Address
Telephone Number
E-mail Address
Gift

Save The Day Card Sent | Invitation Sent | R.S.V.P Received | Thank You Sent | Number Attending

---

Name
Address
Telephone Number
E-mail Address
Gift

Save The Day Card Sent | Invitation Sent | R.S.V.P Received | Thank You Sent | Number Attending

---

Name
Address
Telephone Number
E-mail Address
Gift

Save The Day Card Sent | Invitation Sent | R.S.V.P Received | Thank You Sent | Number Attending

Guest List Planner

Name

Address

Telephone Number

E-mail Address

Gift

| Save The Day Card Sent | Invitation Sent | R.S.V.P Received | Thank You Sent | Number Attending |

Name

Address

Telephone Number

E-mail Address

Gift

| Save The Day Card Sent | Invitation Sent | R.S.V.P Received | Thank You Sent | Number Attending |

Name

Address

Telephone Number

E-mail Address

Gift

| Save The Day Card Sent | Invitation Sent | R.S.V.P Received | Thank You Sent | Number Attending |

Name

Address

Telephone Number

E-mail Address

Gift

| Save The Day Card Sent | Invitation Sent | R.S.V.P Received | Thank You Sent | Number Attending |

Name

Address

Telephone Number

E-mail Address

Gift

| Save The Day Card Sent | Invitation Sent | R.S.V.P Received | Thank You Sent | Number Attending |

Guest List Planner

Name

Address

Telephone Number

E-mail Address

Gift

| Save The Day Card Sent | Invitation Sent | R.S.V.P Received | Thank You Sent | Number Attending |

Name

Address

Telephone Number

E-mail Address

Gift

| Save The Day Card Sent | Invitation Sent | R.S.V.P Received | Thank You Sent | Number Attending |

Name

Address

Telephone Number

E-mail Address

Gift

| Save The Day Card Sent | Invitation Sent | R.S.V.P Received | Thank You Sent | Number Attending |

Name

Address

Telephone Number

E-mail Address

Gift

| Save The Day Card Sent | Invitation Sent | R.S.V.P Received | Thank You Sent | Number Attending |

Name

Address

Telephone Number

E-mail Address

Gift

| Save The Day Card Sent | Invitation Sent | R.S.V.P Received | Thank You Sent | Number Attending |

Guest List Planner

Name

Address

Telephone Number

E-mail Address

Gift

| Save The Day Card Sent | Invitation Sent | R.S.V.P Received | Thank You Sent | Number Attending |

Name

Address

Telephone Number

E-mail Address

Gift

| Save The Day Card Sent | Invitation Sent | R.S.V.P Received | Thank You Sent | Number Attending |

Name

Address

Telephone Number

E-mail Address

Gift

| Save The Day Card Sent | Invitation Sent | R.S.V.P Received | Thank You Sent | Number Attending |

Name

Address

Telephone Number

E-mail Address

Gift

| Save The Day Card Sent | Invitation Sent | R.S.V.P Received | Thank You Sent | Number Attending |

Name

Address

Telephone Number

E-mail Address

Gift

| Save The Day Card Sent | Invitation Sent | R.S.V.P Received | Thank You Sent | Number Attending |

Guest List Planner

Name

Address

Telephone Number

E-mail Address

Gift

| Save The Day Card Sent | Invitation Sent | R.S.V.P Received | Thank You Sent | Number Attending |

Name

Address

Telephone Number

E-mail Address

Gift

| Save The Day Card Sent | Invitation Sent | R.S.V.P Received | Thank You Sent | Number Attending |

Name

Address

Telephone Number

E-mail Address

Gift

| Save The Day Card Sent | Invitation Sent | R.S.V.P Received | Thank You Sent | Number Attending |

Name

Address

Telephone Number

E-mail Address

Gift

| Save The Day Card Sent | Invitation Sent | R.S.V.P Received | Thank You Sent | Number Attending |

Name

Address

Telephone Number

E-mail Address

Gift

| Save The Day Card Sent | Invitation Sent | R.S.V.P Received | Thank You Sent | Number Attending |

Guest List Planner

Name

Address

Telephone Number

E-mail Address

Gift

| Save The Day Card Sent | Invitation Sent | R.S.V.P Received | Thank You Sent | Number Attending |

Name

Address

Telephone Number

E-mail Address

Gift

| Save The Day Card Sent | Invitation Sent | R.S.V.P Received | Thank You Sent | Number Attending |

Name

Address

Telephone Number

E-mail Address

Gift

| Save The Day Card Sent | Invitation Sent | R.S.V.P Received | Thank You Sent | Number Attending |

Name

Address

Telephone Number

E-mail Address

Gift

| Save The Day Card Sent | Invitation Sent | R.S.V.P Received | Thank You Sent | Number Attending |

Name

Address

Telephone Number

E-mail Address

Gift

| Save The Day Card Sent | Invitation Sent | R.S.V.P Received | Thank You Sent | Number Attending |

Guest List Planner

Name
Address
Telephone Number
E-mail Address
Gift

Save The Day Card Sent | Invitation Sent | R.S.V.P Received | Thank You Sent | Number Attending

Name
Address
Telephone Number
E-mail Address
Gift

Save The Day Card Sent | Invitation Sent | R.S.V.P Received | Thank You Sent | Number Attending

Name
Address
Telephone Number
E-mail Address
Gift

Save The Day Card Sent | Invitation Sent | R.S.V.P Received | Thank You Sent | Number Attending

Name
Address
Telephone Number
E-mail Address
Gift

Save The Day Card Sent | Invitation Sent | R.S.V.P Received | Thank You Sent | Number Attending

Name
Address
Telephone Number
E-mail Address
Gift

Save The Day Card Sent | Invitation Sent | R.S.V.P Received | Thank You Sent | Number Attending

Guest List Planner

Name

Address

Telephone Number

E-mail Address

Gift

Save The Day Card Sent | Invitation Sent | R.S.V.P Received | Thank You Sent | Number Attending

---

Name

Address

Telephone Number

E-mail Address

Gift

Save The Day Card Sent | Invitation Sent | R.S.V.P Received | Thank You Sent | Number Attending

---

Name

Address

Telephone Number

E-mail Address

Gift

Save The Day Card Sent | Invitation Sent | R.S.V.P Received | Thank You Sent | Number Attending

---

Name

Address

Telephone Number

E-mail Address

Gift

Save The Day Card Sent | Invitation Sent | R.S.V.P Received | Thank You Sent | Number Attending

---

Name

Address

Telephone Number

E-mail Address

Gift

Save The Day Card Sent | Invitation Sent | R.S.V.P Received | Thank You Sent | Number Attending

Guest List Planner

Name

Address

Telephone Number

E-mail Address

Gift

Save The Day Card Sent	Invitation Sent	R.S.V.P Received	Thank You Sent	Number Attending

Name

Address

Telephone Number

E-mail Address

Gift

Save The Day Card Sent	Invitation Sent	R.S.V.P Received	Thank You Sent	Number Attending

Name

Address

Telephone Number

E-mail Address

Gift

Save The Day Card Sent	Invitation Sent	R.S.V.P Received	Thank You Sent	Number Attending

Name

Address

Telephone Number

E-mail Address

Gift

Save The Day Card Sent	Invitation Sent	R.S.V.P Received	Thank You Sent	Number Attending

Name

Address

Telephone Number

E-mail Address

Gift

Save The Day Card Sent	Invitation Sent	R.S.V.P Received	Thank You Sent	Number Attending

Guest List Planner

Name

Address

Telephone Number

E-mail Address

Gift

| Save The Day Card Sent | Invitation Sent | R.S.V.P Received | Thank You Sent | Number Attending |

Name

Address

Telephone Number

E-mail Address

Gift

| Save The Day Card Sent | Invitation Sent | R.S.V.P Received | Thank You Sent | Number Attending |

Name

Address

Telephone Number

E-mail Address

Gift

| Save The Day Card Sent | Invitation Sent | R.S.V.P Received | Thank You Sent | Number Attending |

Name

Address

Telephone Number

E-mail Address

Gift

| Save The Day Card Sent | Invitation Sent | R.S.V.P Received | Thank You Sent | Number Attending |

Name

Address

Telephone Number

E-mail Address

Gift

| Save The Day Card Sent | Invitation Sent | R.S.V.P Received | Thank You Sent | Number Attending |

Guest List Planner

Name

Address

Telephone Number

E-mail Address

Gift

| Save The Day Card Sent | Invitation Sent | R.S.V.P Received | Thank You Sent | Number Attending |

Name

Address

Telephone Number

E-mail Address

Gift

| Save The Day Card Sent | Invitation Sent | R.S.V.P Received | Thank You Sent | Number Attending |

Name

Address

Telephone Number

E-mail Address

Gift

| Save The Day Card Sent | Invitation Sent | R.S.V.P Received | Thank You Sent | Number Attending |

Name

Address

Telephone Number

E-mail Address

Gift

| Save The Day Card Sent | Invitation Sent | R.S.V.P Received | Thank You Sent | Number Attending |

Name

Address

Telephone Number

E-mail Address

Gift

| Save The Day Card Sent | Invitation Sent | R.S.V.P Received | Thank You Sent | Number Attending |

Guest List Planner

Name

Address

Telephone Number

E-mail Address

Gift

Save The Day Card Sent	Invitation Sent	R.S.V.P Received	Thank You Sent	Number Attending

Name

Address

Telephone Number

E-mail Address

Gift

Save The Day Card Sent	Invitation Sent	R.S.V.P Received	Thank You Sent	Number Attending

Name

Address

Telephone Number

E-mail Address

Gift

Save The Day Card Sent	Invitation Sent	R.S.V.P Received	Thank You Sent	Number Attending

Name

Address

Telephone Number

E-mail Address

Gift

Save The Day Card Sent	Invitation Sent	R.S.V.P Received	Thank You Sent	Number Attending

Name

Address

Telephone Number

E-mail Address

Gift

Save The Day Card Sent	Invitation Sent	R.S.V.P Received	Thank You Sent	Number Attending

Guest List Planner

Name
Address
Telephone Number
E-mail Address
Gift

Save The Day Card Sent | Invitation Sent | R.S.V.P Received | Thank You Sent | Number Attending

---

Name
Address
Telephone Number
E-mail Address
Gift

Save The Day Card Sent | Invitation Sent | R.S.V.P Received | Thank You Sent | Number Attending

---

Name
Address
Telephone Number
E-mail Address
Gift

Save The Day Card Sent | Invitation Sent | R.S.V.P Received | Thank You Sent | Number Attending

---

Name
Address
Telephone Number
E-mail Address
Gift

Save The Day Card Sent | Invitation Sent | R.S.V.P Received | Thank You Sent | Number Attending

---

Name
Address
Telephone Number
E-mail Address
Gift

Save The Day Card Sent | Invitation Sent | R.S.V.P Received | Thank You Sent | Number Attending

Guest List Planner

Name
Address
Telephone Number
E-mail Address
Gift

Save The Day Card Sent | Invitation Sent | R.S.V.P Received | Thank You Sent | Number Attending

Name
Address
Telephone Number
E-mail Address
Gift

Save The Day Card Sent | Invitation Sent | R.S.V.P Received | Thank You Sent | Number Attending

Name
Address
Telephone Number
E-mail Address
Gift

Save The Day Card Sent | Invitation Sent | R.S.V.P Received | Thank You Sent | Number Attending

Name
Address
Telephone Number
E-mail Address
Gift

Save The Day Card Sent | Invitation Sent | R.S.V.P Received | Thank You Sent | Number Attending

Name
Address
Telephone Number
E-mail Address
Gift

Save The Day Card Sent | Invitation Sent | R.S.V.P Received | Thank You Sent | Number Attending

Guest List Planner

Name

Address

Telephone Number

E-mail Address

Gift

| Save The Day Card Sent | Invitation Sent | R.S.V.P Received | Thank You Sent | Number Attending |

Name

Address

Telephone Number

E-mail Address

Gift

| Save The Day Card Sent | Invitation Sent | R.S.V.P Received | Thank You Sent | Number Attending |

Name

Address

Telephone Number

E-mail Address

Gift

| Save The Day Card Sent | Invitation Sent | R.S.V.P Received | Thank You Sent | Number Attending |

Name

Address

Telephone Number

E-mail Address

Gift

| Save The Day Card Sent | Invitation Sent | R.S.V.P Received | Thank You Sent | Number Attending |

Name

Address

Telephone Number

E-mail Address

Gift

| Save The Day Card Sent | Invitation Sent | R.S.V.P Received | Thank You Sent | Number Attending |

Guest List Planner

Name

Address

Telephone Number

E-mail Address

Gift

| Save The Day Card Sent | Invitation Sent | R.S.V.P Received | Thank You Sent | Number Attending |

Name

Address

Telephone Number

E-mail Address

Gift

| Save The Day Card Sent | Invitation Sent | R.S.V.P Received | Thank You Sent | Number Attending |

Name

Address

Telephone Number

E-mail Address

Gift

| Save The Day Card Sent | Invitation Sent | R.S.V.P Received | Thank You Sent | Number Attending |

Name

Address

Telephone Number

E-mail Address

Gift

| Save The Day Card Sent | Invitation Sent | R.S.V.P Received | Thank You Sent | Number Attending |

Name

Address

Telephone Number

E-mail Address

Gift

| Save The Day Card Sent | Invitation Sent | R.S.V.P Received | Thank You Sent | Number Attending |

Guest List Planner

Name

Address

Telephone Number

E-mail Address

Gift

Save The Day Card Sent   Invitation Sent   R.S.V.P Received   Thank You Sent   Number Attending

Name

Address

Telephone Number

E-mail Address

Gift

Save The Day Card Sent   Invitation Sent   R.S.V.P Received   Thank You Sent   Number Attending

Name

Address

Telephone Number

E-mail Address

Gift

Save The Day Card Sent   Invitation Sent   R.S.V.P Received   Thank You Sent   Number Attending

Name

Address

Telephone Number

E-mail Address

Gift

Save The Day Card Sent   Invitation Sent   R.S.V.P Received   Thank You Sent   Number Attending

Name

Address

Telephone Number

E-mail Address

Gift

Save The Day Card Sent   Invitation Sent   R.S.V.P Received   Thank You Sent   Number Attending

Guest List Planner

Name

Address

Telephone Number

E-mail Address

Gift

| Save The Day Card Sent | Invitation Sent | R.S.V.P Received | Thank You Sent | Number Attending |

Name

Address

Telephone Number

E-mail Address

Gift

| Save The Day Card Sent | Invitation Sent | R.S.V.P Received | Thank You Sent | Number Attending |

Name

Address

Telephone Number

E-mail Address

Gift

| Save The Day Card Sent | Invitation Sent | R.S.V.P Received | Thank You Sent | Number Attending |

Name

Address

Telephone Number

E-mail Address

Gift

| Save The Day Card Sent | Invitation Sent | R.S.V.P Received | Thank You Sent | Number Attending |

Name

Address

Telephone Number

E-mail Address

Gift

| Save The Day Card Sent | Invitation Sent | R.S.V.P Received | Thank You Sent | Number Attending |

Guest List Planner

Name

Address

Telephone Number

E-mail Address

Gift

Save The Day Card Sent	Invitation Sent	R.S.V.P Received	Thank You Sent	Number Attending

Name

Address

Telephone Number

E-mail Address

Gift

Save The Day Card Sent	Invitation Sent	R.S.V.P Received	Thank You Sent	Number Attending

Name

Address

Telephone Number

E-mail Address

Gift

Save The Day Card Sent	Invitation Sent	R.S.V.P Received	Thank You Sent	Number Attending

Name

Address

Telephone Number

E-mail Address

Gift

Save The Day Card Sent	Invitation Sent	R.S.V.P Received	Thank You Sent	Number Attending

Name

Address

Telephone Number

E-mail Address

Gift

Save The Day Card Sent	Invitation Sent	R.S.V.P Received	Thank You Sent	Number Attending

Guest List Planner

Name
Address
Telephone Number
E-mail Address
Gift

Save The Day Card Sent | Invitation Sent | R.S.V.P Received | Thank You Sent | Number Attending

Name
Address
Telephone Number
E-mail Address
Gift

Save The Day Card Sent | Invitation Sent | R.S.V.P Received | Thank You Sent | Number Attending

Name
Address
Telephone Number
E-mail Address
Gift

Save The Day Card Sent | Invitation Sent | R.S.V.P Received | Thank You Sent | Number Attending

Name
Address
Telephone Number
E-mail Address
Gift

Save The Day Card Sent | Invitation Sent | R.S.V.P Received | Thank You Sent | Number Attending

Name
Address
Telephone Number
E-mail Address
Gift

Save The Day Card Sent | Invitation Sent | R.S.V.P Received | Thank You Sent | Number Attending

Guest List Planner

Name

Address

Telephone Number

E-mail Address

Gift

| Save The Day Card Sent | Invitation Sent | R.S.V.P Received | Thank You Sent | Number Attending |

Name

Address

Telephone Number

E-mail Address

Gift

| Save The Day Card Sent | Invitation Sent | R.S.V.P Received | Thank You Sent | Number Attending |

Name

Address

Telephone Number

E-mail Address

Gift

| Save The Day Card Sent | Invitation Sent | R.S.V.P Received | Thank You Sent | Number Attending |

Name

Address

Telephone Number

E-mail Address

Gift

| Save The Day Card Sent | Invitation Sent | R.S.V.P Received | Thank You Sent | Number Attending |

Name

Address

Telephone Number

E-mail Address

Gift

| Save The Day Card Sent | Invitation Sent | R.S.V.P Received | Thank You Sent | Number Attending |

Guest List Planner

Name

Address

Telephone Number

E-mail Address

Gift

| Save The Day Card Sent | Invitation Sent | R.S.V.P Received | Thank You Sent | Number Attending |

Name

Address

Telephone Number

E-mail Address

Gift

| Save The Day Card Sent | Invitation Sent | R.S.V.P Received | Thank You Sent | Number Attending |

Name

Address

Telephone Number

E-mail Address

Gift

| Save The Day Card Sent | Invitation Sent | R.S.V.P Received | Thank You Sent | Number Attending |

Name

Address

Telephone Number

E-mail Address

Gift

| Save The Day Card Sent | Invitation Sent | R.S.V.P Received | Thank You Sent | Number Attending |

Name

Address

Telephone Number

E-mail Address

Gift

| Save The Day Card Sent | Invitation Sent | R.S.V.P Received | Thank You Sent | Number Attending |

Guest List Planner

Name

Address

Telephone Number

E-mail Address

Gift

Save The Day Card Sent	Invitation Sent	R.S.V.P Received	Thank You Sent	Number Attending

Name

Address

Telephone Number

E-mail Address

Gift

Save The Day Card Sent	Invitation Sent	R.S.V.P Received	Thank You Sent	Number Attending

Name

Address

Telephone Number

E-mail Address

Gift

Save The Day Card Sent	Invitation Sent	R.S.V.P Received	Thank You Sent	Number Attending

Name

Address

Telephone Number

E-mail Address

Gift

Save The Day Card Sent	Invitation Sent	R.S.V.P Received	Thank You Sent	Number Attending

Name

Address

Telephone Number

E-mail Address

Gift

Save The Day Card Sent	Invitation Sent	R.S.V.P Received	Thank You Sent	Number Attending

Guest List Planner

Name

Address

Telephone Number

E-mail Address

Gift

| Save The Day Card Sent | Invitation Sent | R.S.V.P Received | Thank You Sent | Number Attending |

Name

Address

Telephone Number

E-mail Address

Gift

| Save The Day Card Sent | Invitation Sent | R.S.V.P Received | Thank You Sent | Number Attending |

Name

Address

Telephone Number

E-mail Address

Gift

| Save The Day Card Sent | Invitation Sent | R.S.V.P Received | Thank You Sent | Number Attending |

Name

Address

Telephone Number

E-mail Address

Gift

| Save The Day Card Sent | Invitation Sent | R.S.V.P Received | Thank You Sent | Number Attending |

Name

Address

Telephone Number

E-mail Address

Gift

| Save The Day Card Sent | Invitation Sent | R.S.V.P Received | Thank You Sent | Number Attending |

Guest List Planner

Name

Address

Telephone Number

E-mail Address

Gift

Save The Day Card Sent   Invitation Sent   R.S.V.P Received   Thank You Sent   Number Attending

Name

Address

Telephone Number

E-mail Address

Gift

Save The Day Card Sent   Invitation Sent   R.S.V.P Received   Thank You Sent   Number Attending

Name

Address

Telephone Number

E-mail Address

Gift

Save The Day Card Sent   Invitation Sent   R.S.V.P Received   Thank You Sent   Number Attending

Name

Address

Telephone Number

E-mail Address

Gift

Save The Day Card Sent   Invitation Sent   R.S.V.P Received   Thank You Sent   Number Attending

Name

Address

Telephone Number

E-mail Address

Gift

Save The Day Card Sent   Invitation Sent   R.S.V.P Received   Thank You Sent   Number Attending

Guest List Planner

Name

Address

Telephone Number

E-mail Address

Gift

| Save The Day Card Sent | Invitation Sent | R.S.V.P Received | Thank You Sent | Number Attending |

Name

Address

Telephone Number

E-mail Address

Gift

| Save The Day Card Sent | Invitation Sent | R.S.V.P Received | Thank You Sent | Number Attending |

Name

Address

Telephone Number

E-mail Address

Gift

| Save The Day Card Sent | Invitation Sent | R.S.V.P Received | Thank You Sent | Number Attending |

Name

Address

Telephone Number

E-mail Address

Gift

| Save The Day Card Sent | Invitation Sent | R.S.V.P Received | Thank You Sent | Number Attending |

Name

Address

Telephone Number

E-mail Address

Gift

| Save The Day Card Sent | Invitation Sent | R.S.V.P Received | Thank You Sent | Number Attending |

Guest List Planner

Name

Address

Telephone Number

E-mail Address

Gift

Save The Day Card Sent	Invitation Sent	R.S.V.P Received	Thank You Sent	Number Attending

Name

Address

Telephone Number

E-mail Address

Gift

Save The Day Card Sent	Invitation Sent	R.S.V.P Received	Thank You Sent	Number Attending

Name

Address

Telephone Number

E-mail Address

Gift

Save The Day Card Sent	Invitation Sent	R.S.V.P Received	Thank You Sent	Number Attending

Name

Address

Telephone Number

E-mail Address

Gift

Save The Day Card Sent	Invitation Sent	R.S.V.P Received	Thank You Sent	Number Attending

Name

Address

Telephone Number

E-mail Address

Gift

Save The Day Card Sent	Invitation Sent	R.S.V.P Received	Thank You Sent	Number Attending

Guest List Planner

Name

Address

Telephone Number

E-mail Address

Gift

Save The Day Card Sent	Invitation Sent	R.S.V.P Received	Thank You Sent	Number Attending

Name

Address

Telephone Number

E-mail Address

Gift

Save The Day Card Sent	Invitation Sent	R.S.V.P Received	Thank You Sent	Number Attending

Name

Address

Telephone Number

E-mail Address

Gift

Save The Day Card Sent	Invitation Sent	R.S.V.P Received	Thank You Sent	Number Attending

Name

Address

Telephone Number

E-mail Address

Gift

Save The Day Card Sent	Invitation Sent	R.S.V.P Received	Thank You Sent	Number Attending

Name

Address

Telephone Number

E-mail Address

Gift

Save The Day Card Sent	Invitation Sent	R.S.V.P Received	Thank You Sent	Number Attending

Guest List Planner

Name

Address

Telephone Number

E-mail Address

Gift

Save The Day Card Sent	Invitation Sent	R.S.V.P Received	Thank You Sent	Number Attending

Name

Address

Telephone Number

E-mail Address

Gift

Save The Day Card Sent	Invitation Sent	R.S.V.P Received	Thank You Sent	Number Attending

Name

Address

Telephone Number

E-mail Address

Gift

Save The Day Card Sent	Invitation Sent	R.S.V.P Received	Thank You Sent	Number Attending

Name

Address

Telephone Number

E-mail Address

Gift

Save The Day Card Sent	Invitation Sent	R.S.V.P Received	Thank You Sent	Number Attending

Name

Address

Telephone Number

E-mail Address

Gift

Save The Day Card Sent	Invitation Sent	R.S.V.P Received	Thank You Sent	Number Attending

Guest List Planner

Name

Address

Telephone Number

E-mail Address

Gift

| Save The Day Card Sent | Invitation Sent | R.S.V.P Received | Thank You Sent | Number Attending |

Name

Address

Telephone Number

E-mail Address

Gift

| Save The Day Card Sent | Invitation Sent | R.S.V.P Received | Thank You Sent | Number Attending |

Name

Address

Telephone Number

E-mail Address

Gift

| Save The Day Card Sent | Invitation Sent | R.S.V.P Received | Thank You Sent | Number Attending |

Name

Address

Telephone Number

E-mail Address

Gift

| Save The Day Card Sent | Invitation Sent | R.S.V.P Received | Thank You Sent | Number Attending |

Name

Address

Telephone Number

E-mail Address

Gift

| Save The Day Card Sent | Invitation Sent | R.S.V.P Received | Thank You Sent | Number Attending |

Guest List Planner

Name

Address

Telephone Number

E-mail Address

Gift

Save The Day Card Sent	Invitation Sent	R.S.V.P Received	Thank You Sent	Number Attending

Name

Address

Telephone Number

E-mail Address

Gift

Save The Day Card Sent	Invitation Sent	R.S.V.P Received	Thank You Sent	Number Attending

Name

Address

Telephone Number

E-mail Address

Gift

Save The Day Card Sent	Invitation Sent	R.S.V.P Received	Thank You Sent	Number Attending

Name

Address

Telephone Number

E-mail Address

Gift

Save The Day Card Sent	Invitation Sent	R.S.V.P Received	Thank You Sent	Number Attending

Name

Address

Telephone Number

E-mail Address

Gift

Save The Day Card Sent	Invitation Sent	R.S.V.P Received	Thank You Sent	Number Attending

Guest List Planner

Name

Address

Telephone Number

E-mail Address

Gift

Save The Day Card Sent	Invitation Sent	R.S.V.P Received	Thank You Sent	Number Attending

Name

Address

Telephone Number

E-mail Address

Gift

Save The Day Card Sent	Invitation Sent	R.S.V.P Received	Thank You Sent	Number Attending

Name

Address

Telephone Number

E-mail Address

Gift

Save The Day Card Sent	Invitation Sent	R.S.V.P Received	Thank You Sent	Number Attending

Name

Address

Telephone Number

E-mail Address

Gift

Save The Day Card Sent	Invitation Sent	R.S.V.P Received	Thank You Sent	Number Attending

Name

Address

Telephone Number

E-mail Address

Gift

Save The Day Card Sent	Invitation Sent	R.S.V.P Received	Thank You Sent	Number Attending

Guest List Planner

Name

Address

Telephone Number

E-mail Address

Gift

Save The Day   Invitation   R.S.V.P   Thank You   Number
Card Sent   Sent   Received   Sent   Attending

Name

Address

Telephone Number

E-mail Address

Gift

Save The Day   Invitation   R.S.V.P   Thank You   Number
Card Sent   Sent   Received   Sent   Attending

Name

Address

Telephone Number

E-mail Address

Gift

Save The Day   Invitation   R.S.V.P   Thank You   Number
Card Sent   Sent   Received   Sent   Attending

Name

Address

Telephone Number

E-mail Address

Gift

Save The Day   Invitation   R.S.V.P   Thank You   Number
Card Sent   Sent   Received   Sent   Attending

Name

Address

Telephone Number

E-mail Address

Gift

Save The Day   Invitation   R.S.V.P   Thank You   Number
Card Sent   Sent   Received   Sent   Attending

Guest List Planner

Name

Address

Telephone Number

E-mail Address

Gift

| Save The Day Card Sent | Invitation Sent | R.S.V.P Received | Thank You Sent | Number Attending |

Name

Address

Telephone Number

E-mail Address

Gift

| Save The Day Card Sent | Invitation Sent | R.S.V.P Received | Thank You Sent | Number Attending |

Name

Address

Telephone Number

E-mail Address

Gift

| Save The Day Card Sent | Invitation Sent | R.S.V.P Received | Thank You Sent | Number Attending |

Name

Address

Telephone Number

E-mail Address

Gift

| Save The Day Card Sent | Invitation Sent | R.S.V.P Received | Thank You Sent | Number Attending |

Name

Address

Telephone Number

E-mail Address

Gift

| Save The Day Card Sent | Invitation Sent | R.S.V.P Received | Thank You Sent | Number Attending |

Guest List Planner

Name

Address

Telephone Number

E-mail Address

Gift

| Save The Day Card Sent | Invitation Sent | R.S.V.P Received | Thank You Sent | Number Attending |

Name

Address

Telephone Number

E-mail Address

Gift

| Save The Day Card Sent | Invitation Sent | R.S.V.P Received | Thank You Sent | Number Attending |

Name

Address

Telephone Number

E-mail Address

Gift

| Save The Day Card Sent | Invitation Sent | R.S.V.P Received | Thank You Sent | Number Attending |

Name

Address

Telephone Number

E-mail Address

Gift

| Save The Day Card Sent | Invitation Sent | R.S.V.P Received | Thank You Sent | Number Attending |

Name

Address

Telephone Number

E-mail Address

Gift

| Save The Day Card Sent | Invitation Sent | R.S.V.P Received | Thank You Sent | Number Attending |

Guest List Planner

Name

Address

Telephone Number

E-mail Address

Gift

Save The Day Card Sent	Invitation Sent	R.S.V.P Received	Thank You Sent	Number Attending

Name

Address

Telephone Number

E-mail Address

Gift

Save The Day Card Sent	Invitation Sent	R.S.V.P Received	Thank You Sent	Number Attending

Name

Address

Telephone Number

E-mail Address

Gift

Save The Day Card Sent	Invitation Sent	R.S.V.P Received	Thank You Sent	Number Attending

Name

Address

Telephone Number

E-mail Address

Gift

Save The Day Card Sent	Invitation Sent	R.S.V.P Received	Thank You Sent	Number Attending

Name

Address

Telephone Number

E-mail Address

Gift

Save The Day Card Sent	Invitation Sent	R.S.V.P Received	Thank You Sent	Number Attending

Guest List Planner

Name

Address

Telephone Number

E-mail Address

Gift

| Save The Day Card Sent | Invitation Sent | R.S.V.P Received | Thank You Sent | Number Attending |

Name

Address

Telephone Number

E-mail Address

Gift

| Save The Day Card Sent | Invitation Sent | R.S.V.P Received | Thank You Sent | Number Attending |

Name

Address

Telephone Number

E-mail Address

Gift

| Save The Day Card Sent | Invitation Sent | R.S.V.P Received | Thank You Sent | Number Attending |

Name

Address

Telephone Number

E-mail Address

Gift

| Save The Day Card Sent | Invitation Sent | R.S.V.P Received | Thank You Sent | Number Attending |

Name

Address

Telephone Number

E-mail Address

Gift

| Save The Day Card Sent | Invitation Sent | R.S.V.P Received | Thank You Sent | Number Attending |

Guest List Planner

Name

Address

Telephone Number

E-mail Address

Gift

| Save The Day Card Sent | Invitation Sent | R.S.V.P Received | Thank You Sent | Number Attending |

Name

Address

Telephone Number

E-mail Address

Gift

| Save The Day Card Sent | Invitation Sent | R.S.V.P Received | Thank You Sent | Number Attending |

Name

Address

Telephone Number

E-mail Address

Gift

| Save The Day Card Sent | Invitation Sent | R.S.V.P Received | Thank You Sent | Number Attending |

Name

Address

Telephone Number

E-mail Address

Gift

| Save The Day Card Sent | Invitation Sent | R.S.V.P Received | Thank You Sent | Number Attending |

Name

Address

Telephone Number

E-mail Address

Gift

| Save The Day Card Sent | Invitation Sent | R.S.V.P Received | Thank You Sent | Number Attending |

Guest List Planner

Name

Address

Telephone Number

E-mail Address

Gift

Save The Day Card Sent	Invitation Sent	R.S.V.P Received	Thank You Sent	Number Attending

Name

Address

Telephone Number

E-mail Address

Gift

Save The Day Card Sent	Invitation Sent	R.S.V.P Received	Thank You Sent	Number Attending

Name

Address

Telephone Number

E-mail Address

Gift

Save The Day Card Sent	Invitation Sent	R.S.V.P Received	Thank You Sent	Number Attending

Name

Address

Telephone Number

E-mail Address

Gift

Save The Day Card Sent	Invitation Sent	R.S.V.P Received	Thank You Sent	Number Attending

Name

Address

Telephone Number

E-mail Address

Gift

Save The Day Card Sent	Invitation Sent	R.S.V.P Received	Thank You Sent	Number Attending

Guest List Planner

Name

Address

Telephone Number

E-mail Address

Gift

Save The Day Card Sent	Invitation Sent	R.S.V.P Received	Thank You Sent	Number Attending

Name

Address

Telephone Number

E-mail Address

Gift

Save The Day Card Sent	Invitation Sent	R.S.V.P Received	Thank You Sent	Number Attending

Name

Address

Telephone Number

E-mail Address

Gift

Save The Day Card Sent	Invitation Sent	R.S.V.P Received	Thank You Sent	Number Attending

Name

Address

Telephone Number

E-mail Address

Gift

Save The Day Card Sent	Invitation Sent	R.S.V.P Received	Thank You Sent	Number Attending

Name

Address

Telephone Number

E-mail Address

Gift

Save The Day Card Sent	Invitation Sent	R.S.V.P Received	Thank You Sent	Number Attending

Guest List Planner

Name

Address

Telephone Number

E-mail Address

Gift

Save The Day Card Sent	Invitation Sent	R.S.V.P Received	Thank You Sent	Number Attending

Name

Address

Telephone Number

E-mail Address

Gift

Save The Day Card Sent	Invitation Sent	R.S.V.P Received	Thank You Sent	Number Attending

Name

Address

Telephone Number

E-mail Address

Gift

Save The Day Card Sent	Invitation Sent	R.S.V.P Received	Thank You Sent	Number Attending

Name

Address

Telephone Number

E-mail Address

Gift

Save The Day Card Sent	Invitation Sent	R.S.V.P Received	Thank You Sent	Number Attending

Name

Address

Telephone Number

E-mail Address

Gift

Save The Day Card Sent	Invitation Sent	R.S.V.P Received	Thank You Sent	Number Attending

Guest List Planner

Name

Address

Telephone Number

E-mail Address

Gift

| Save The Day Card Sent | Invitation Sent | R.S.V.P Received | Thank You Sent | Number Attending |

Name

Address

Telephone Number

E-mail Address

Gift

| Save The Day Card Sent | Invitation Sent | R.S.V.P Received | Thank You Sent | Number Attending |

Name

Address

Telephone Number

E-mail Address

Gift

| Save The Day Card Sent | Invitation Sent | R.S.V.P Received | Thank You Sent | Number Attending |

Name

Address

Telephone Number

E-mail Address

Gift

| Save The Day Card Sent | Invitation Sent | R.S.V.P Received | Thank You Sent | Number Attending |

Name

Address

Telephone Number

E-mail Address

Gift

| Save The Day Card Sent | Invitation Sent | R.S.V.P Received | Thank You Sent | Number Attending |

Guest List Planner

Name
Address
Telephone Number
E-mail Address
Gift

Save The Day Card Sent | Invitation Sent | R.S.V.P Received | Thank You Sent | Number Attending

Name
Address
Telephone Number
E-mail Address
Gift

Save The Day Card Sent | Invitation Sent | R.S.V.P Received | Thank You Sent | Number Attending

Name
Address
Telephone Number
E-mail Address
Gift

Save The Day Card Sent | Invitation Sent | R.S.V.P Received | Thank You Sent | Number Attending

Name
Address
Telephone Number
E-mail Address
Gift

Save The Day Card Sent | Invitation Sent | R.S.V.P Received | Thank You Sent | Number Attending

Name
Address
Telephone Number
E-mail Address
Gift

Save The Day Card Sent | Invitation Sent | R.S.V.P Received | Thank You Sent | Number Attending

Guest List Planner

Name

Address

Telephone Number

E-mail Address

Gift

| Save The Day Card Sent | Invitation Sent | R.S.V.P Received | Thank You Sent | Number Attending |

Name

Address

Telephone Number

E-mail Address

Gift

| Save The Day Card Sent | Invitation Sent | R.S.V.P Received | Thank You Sent | Number Attending |

Name

Address

Telephone Number

E-mail Address

Gift

| Save The Day Card Sent | Invitation Sent | R.S.V.P Received | Thank You Sent | Number Attending |

Name

Address

Telephone Number

E-mail Address

Gift

| Save The Day Card Sent | Invitation Sent | R.S.V.P Received | Thank You Sent | Number Attending |

Name

Address

Telephone Number

E-mail Address

Gift

| Save The Day Card Sent | Invitation Sent | R.S.V.P Received | Thank You Sent | Number Attending |

Guest List Planner

Name

Address

Telephone Number

E-mail Address

Gift

| Save The Day Card Sent | Invitation Sent | R.S.V.P Received | Thank You Sent | Number Attending |

Name

Address

Telephone Number

E-mail Address

Gift

| Save The Day Card Sent | Invitation Sent | R.S.V.P Received | Thank You Sent | Number Attending |

Name

Address

Telephone Number

E-mail Address

Gift

| Save The Day Card Sent | Invitation Sent | R.S.V.P Received | Thank You Sent | Number Attending |

Name

Address

Telephone Number

E-mail Address

Gift

| Save The Day Card Sent | Invitation Sent | R.S.V.P Received | Thank You Sent | Number Attending |

Name

Address

Telephone Number

E-mail Address

Gift

| Save The Day Card Sent | Invitation Sent | R.S.V.P Received | Thank You Sent | Number Attending |

Guest List Planner

Name

Address

Telephone Number

E-mail Address

Gift

| Save The Day Card Sent | Invitation Sent | R.S.V.P Received | Thank You Sent | Number Attending |

Name

Address

Telephone Number

E-mail Address

Gift

| Save The Day Card Sent | Invitation Sent | R.S.V.P Received | Thank You Sent | Number Attending |

Name

Address

Telephone Number

E-mail Address

Gift

| Save The Day Card Sent | Invitation Sent | R.S.V.P Received | Thank You Sent | Number Attending |

Name

Address

Telephone Number

E-mail Address

Gift

| Save The Day Card Sent | Invitation Sent | R.S.V.P Received | Thank You Sent | Number Attending |

Name

Address

Telephone Number

E-mail Address

Gift

| Save The Day Card Sent | Invitation Sent | R.S.V.P Received | Thank You Sent | Number Attending |

Guest List Planner

Name

Address

Telephone Number

E-mail Address

Gift

| Save The Day Card Sent | Invitation Sent | R.S.V.P Received | Thank You Sent | Number Attending |

Name

Address

Telephone Number

E-mail Address

Gift

| Save The Day Card Sent | Invitation Sent | R.S.V.P Received | Thank You Sent | Number Attending |

Name

Address

Telephone Number

E-mail Address

Gift

| Save The Day Card Sent | Invitation Sent | R.S.V.P Received | Thank You Sent | Number Attending |

Name

Address

Telephone Number

E-mail Address

Gift

| Save The Day Card Sent | Invitation Sent | R.S.V.P Received | Thank You Sent | Number Attending |

Name

Address

Telephone Number

E-mail Address

Gift

| Save The Day Card Sent | Invitation Sent | R.S.V.P Received | Thank You Sent | Number Attending |

Guest List Planner

Name
Address
Telephone Number
E-mail Address
Gift

Save The Day Card Sent | Invitation Sent | R.S.V.P Received | Thank You Sent | Number Attending

Name
Address
Telephone Number
E-mail Address
Gift

Save The Day Card Sent | Invitation Sent | R.S.V.P Received | Thank You Sent | Number Attending

Name
Address
Telephone Number
E-mail Address
Gift

Save The Day Card Sent | Invitation Sent | R.S.V.P Received | Thank You Sent | Number Attending

Name
Address
Telephone Number
E-mail Address
Gift

Save The Day Card Sent | Invitation Sent | R.S.V.P Received | Thank You Sent | Number Attending

Name
Address
Telephone Number
E-mail Address
Gift

Save The Day Card Sent | Invitation Sent | R.S.V.P Received | Thank You Sent | Number Attending

Guest List Planner

Name

Address

Telephone Number

E-mail Address

Gift

Save The Day Card Sent   Invitation Sent   R.S.V.P Received   Thank You Sent   Number Attending

Name

Address

Telephone Number

E-mail Address

Gift

Save The Day Card Sent   Invitation Sent   R.S.V.P Received   Thank You Sent   Number Attending

Name

Address

Telephone Number

E-mail Address

Gift

Save The Day Card Sent   Invitation Sent   R.S.V.P Received   Thank You Sent   Number Attending

Name

Address

Telephone Number

E-mail Address

Gift

Save The Day Card Sent   Invitation Sent   R.S.V.P Received   Thank You Sent   Number Attending

Name

Address

Telephone Number

E-mail Address

Gift

Save The Day Card Sent   Invitation Sent   R.S.V.P Received   Thank You Sent   Number Attending

Guest List Planner

Name

Address

Telephone Number

E-mail Address

Gift

| Save The Day Card Sent | Invitation Sent | R.S.V.P Received | Thank You Sent | Number Attending |

Name

Address

Telephone Number

E-mail Address

Gift

| Save The Day Card Sent | Invitation Sent | R.S.V.P Received | Thank You Sent | Number Attending |

Name

Address

Telephone Number

E-mail Address

Gift

| Save The Day Card Sent | Invitation Sent | R.S.V.P Received | Thank You Sent | Number Attending |

Name

Address

Telephone Number

E-mail Address

Gift

| Save The Day Card Sent | Invitation Sent | R.S.V.P Received | Thank You Sent | Number Attending |

Name

Address

Telephone Number

E-mail Address

Gift

| Save The Day Card Sent | Invitation Sent | R.S.V.P Received | Thank You Sent | Number Attending |

Guest List Planner

Name

Address

Telephone Number

E-mail Address

Gift

Save The Day Card Sent   Invitation Sent   R.S.V.P Received   Thank You Sent   Number Attending

Name

Address

Telephone Number

E-mail Address

Gift

Save The Day Card Sent   Invitation Sent   R.S.V.P Received   Thank You Sent   Number Attending

Name

Address

Telephone Number

E-mail Address

Gift

Save The Day Card Sent   Invitation Sent   R.S.V.P Received   Thank You Sent   Number Attending

Name

Address

Telephone Number

E-mail Address

Gift

Save The Day Card Sent   Invitation Sent   R.S.V.P Received   Thank You Sent   Number Attending

Name

Address

Telephone Number

E-mail Address

Gift

Save The Day Card Sent   Invitation Sent   R.S.V.P Received   Thank You Sent   Number Attending

Guest List Planner

Name

Address

Telephone Number

E-mail Address

Gift

| Save The Day Card Sent | Invitation Sent | R.S.V.P Received | Thank You Sent | Number Attending |

Name

Address

Telephone Number

E-mail Address

Gift

| Save The Day Card Sent | Invitation Sent | R.S.V.P Received | Thank You Sent | Number Attending |

Name

Address

Telephone Number

E-mail Address

Gift

| Save The Day Card Sent | Invitation Sent | R.S.V.P Received | Thank You Sent | Number Attending |

Name

Address

Telephone Number

E-mail Address

Gift

| Save The Day Card Sent | Invitation Sent | R.S.V.P Received | Thank You Sent | Number Attending |

Name

Address

Telephone Number

E-mail Address

Gift

| Save The Day Card Sent | Invitation Sent | R.S.V.P Received | Thank You Sent | Number Attending |

Guest List Planner

Name

Address

Telephone Number

E-mail Address

Gift

Save The Day Card Sent　　　Invitation Sent　　　R.S.V.P Received　　　Thank You Sent　　　Number Attending

Name

Address

Telephone Number

E-mail Address

Gift

Save The Day Card Sent　　　Invitation Sent　　　R.S.V.P Received　　　Thank You Sent　　　Number Attending

Name

Address

Telephone Number

E-mail Address

Gift

Save The Day Card Sent　　　Invitation Sent　　　R.S.V.P Received　　　Thank You Sent　　　Number Attending

Name

Address

Telephone Number

E-mail Address

Gift

Save The Day Card Sent　　　Invitation Sent　　　R.S.V.P Received　　　Thank You Sent　　　Number Attending

Name

Address

Telephone Number

E-mail Address

Gift

Save The Day Card Sent　　　Invitation Sent　　　R.S.V.P Received　　　Thank You Sent　　　Number Attending

Guest List Planner

Name

Address

Telephone Number

E-mail Address

Gift

| Save The Day Card Sent | Invitation Sent | R.S.V.P Received | Thank You Sent | Number Attending |

Name

Address

Telephone Number

E-mail Address

Gift

| Save The Day Card Sent | Invitation Sent | R.S.V.P Received | Thank You Sent | Number Attending |

Name

Address

Telephone Number

E-mail Address

Gift

| Save The Day Card Sent | Invitation Sent | R.S.V.P Received | Thank You Sent | Number Attending |

Name

Address

Telephone Number

E-mail Address

Gift

| Save The Day Card Sent | Invitation Sent | R.S.V.P Received | Thank You Sent | Number Attending |

Name

Address

Telephone Number

E-mail Address

Gift

| Save The Day Card Sent | Invitation Sent | R.S.V.P Received | Thank You Sent | Number Attending |

Guest List Planner

Name
Address
Telephone Number
E-mail Address
Gift

Save The Day Card Sent | Invitation Sent | R.S.V.P Received | Thank You Sent | Number Attending

Name
Address
Telephone Number
E-mail Address
Gift

Save The Day Card Sent | Invitation Sent | R.S.V.P Received | Thank You Sent | Number Attending

Name
Address
Telephone Number
E-mail Address
Gift

Save The Day Card Sent | Invitation Sent | R.S.V.P Received | Thank You Sent | Number Attending

Name
Address
Telephone Number
E-mail Address
Gift

Save The Day Card Sent | Invitation Sent | R.S.V.P Received | Thank You Sent | Number Attending

Name
Address
Telephone Number
E-mail Address
Gift

Save The Day Card Sent | Invitation Sent | R.S.V.P Received | Thank You Sent | Number Attending

Guest List Planner

Name

Address

Telephone Number

E-mail Address

Gift

Save The Day Card Sent   Invitation Sent   R.S.V.P Received   Thank You Sent   Number Attending

Name

Address

Telephone Number

E-mail Address

Gift

Save The Day Card Sent   Invitation Sent   R.S.V.P Received   Thank You Sent   Number Attending

Name

Address

Telephone Number

E-mail Address

Gift

Save The Day Card Sent   Invitation Sent   R.S.V.P Received   Thank You Sent   Number Attending

Name

Address

Telephone Number

E-mail Address

Gift

Save The Day Card Sent   Invitation Sent   R.S.V.P Received   Thank You Sent   Number Attending

Name

Address

Telephone Number

E-mail Address

Gift

Save The Day Card Sent   Invitation Sent   R.S.V.P Received   Thank You Sent   Number Attending

Guest List Planner

Name

Address

Telephone Number

E-mail Address

Gift

Save The Day Card Sent	Invitation Sent	R.S.V.P Received	Thank You Sent	Number Attending

Name

Address

Telephone Number

E-mail Address

Gift

Save The Day Card Sent	Invitation Sent	R.S.V.P Received	Thank You Sent	Number Attending

Name

Address

Telephone Number

E-mail Address

Gift

Save The Day Card Sent	Invitation Sent	R.S.V.P Received	Thank You Sent	Number Attending

Name

Address

Telephone Number

E-mail Address

Gift

Save The Day Card Sent	Invitation Sent	R.S.V.P Received	Thank You Sent	Number Attending

Name

Address

Telephone Number

E-mail Address

Gift

Save The Day Card Sent	Invitation Sent	R.S.V.P Received	Thank You Sent	Number Attending

Guest List Planner

Name

Address

Telephone Number

E-mail Address

Gift

| Save The Day Card Sent | Invitation Sent | R.S.V.P Received | Thank You Sent | Number Attending |

Name

Address

Telephone Number

E-mail Address

Gift

| Save The Day Card Sent | Invitation Sent | R.S.V.P Received | Thank You Sent | Number Attending |

Name

Address

Telephone Number

E-mail Address

Gift

| Save The Day Card Sent | Invitation Sent | R.S.V.P Received | Thank You Sent | Number Attending |

Name

Address

Telephone Number

E-mail Address

Gift

| Save The Day Card Sent | Invitation Sent | R.S.V.P Received | Thank You Sent | Number Attending |

Name

Address

Telephone Number

E-mail Address

Gift

| Save The Day Card Sent | Invitation Sent | R.S.V.P Received | Thank You Sent | Number Attending |

Guest List Planner

Name

Address

Telephone Number

E-mail Address

Gift

Save The Day Card Sent   Invitation Sent   R.S.V.P Received   Thank You Sent   Number Attending

Name

Address

Telephone Number

E-mail Address

Gift

Save The Day Card Sent   Invitation Sent   R.S.V.P Received   Thank You Sent   Number Attending

Name

Address

Telephone Number

E-mail Address

Gift

Save The Day Card Sent   Invitation Sent   R.S.V.P Received   Thank You Sent   Number Attending

Name

Address

Telephone Number

E-mail Address

Gift

Save The Day Card Sent   Invitation Sent   R.S.V.P Received   Thank You Sent   Number Attending

Name

Address

Telephone Number

E-mail Address

Gift

Save The Day Card Sent   Invitation Sent   R.S.V.P Received   Thank You Sent   Number Attending

Guest List Planner

Name

Address

Telephone Number

E-mail Address

Gift

Save The Day Card Sent   Invitation Sent   R.S.V.P Received   Thank You Sent   Number Attending

Name

Address

Telephone Number

E-mail Address

Gift

Save The Day Card Sent   Invitation Sent   R.S.V.P Received   Thank You Sent   Number Attending

Name

Address

Telephone Number

E-mail Address

Gift

Save The Day Card Sent   Invitation Sent   R.S.V.P Received   Thank You Sent   Number Attending

Name

Address

Telephone Number

E-mail Address

Gift

Save The Day Card Sent   Invitation Sent   R.S.V.P Received   Thank You Sent   Number Attending

Name

Address

Telephone Number

E-mail Address

Gift

Save The Day Card Sent   Invitation Sent   R.S.V.P Received   Thank You Sent   Number Attending

Guest List Planner

Name

Address

Telephone Number

E-mail Address

Gift

Save The Day Invitation R.S.V.P Thank You Number
Card Sent Sent Received Sent Attending

Name

Address

Telephone Number

E-mail Address

Gift

Save The Day Invitation R.S.V.P Thank You Number
Card Sent Sent Received Sent Attending

Name

Address

Telephone Number

E-mail Address

Gift

Save The Day Invitation R.S.V.P Thank You Number
Card Sent Sent Received Sent Attending

Name

Address

Telephone Number

E-mail Address

Gift

Save The Day Invitation R.S.V.P Thank You Number
Card Sent Sent Received Sent Attending

Name

Address

Telephone Number

E-mail Address

Gift

Save The Day Invitation R.S.V.P Thank You Number
Card Sent Sent Received Sent Attending

Guest List Planner

Name

Address

Telephone Number

E-mail Address

Gift

| Save The Day Card Sent | Invitation Sent | R.S.V.P Received | Thank You Sent | Number Attending |

Name

Address

Telephone Number

E-mail Address

Gift

| Save The Day Card Sent | Invitation Sent | R.S.V.P Received | Thank You Sent | Number Attending |

Name

Address

Telephone Number

E-mail Address

Gift

| Save The Day Card Sent | Invitation Sent | R.S.V.P Received | Thank You Sent | Number Attending |

Name

Address

Telephone Number

E-mail Address

Gift

| Save The Day Card Sent | Invitation Sent | R.S.V.P Received | Thank You Sent | Number Attending |

Name

Address

Telephone Number

E-mail Address

Gift

| Save The Day Card Sent | Invitation Sent | R.S.V.P Received | Thank You Sent | Number Attending |

Guest List Planner

Name

Address

Telephone Number

E-mail Address

Gift

Save The Day   Invitation   R.S.V.P   Thank You   Number
Card Sent   Sent   Received   Sent   Attending

Name

Address

Telephone Number

E-mail Address

Gift

Save The Day   Invitation   R.S.V.P   Thank You   Number
Card Sent   Sent   Received   Sent   Attending

Name

Address

Telephone Number

E-mail Address

Gift

Save The Day   Invitation   R.S.V.P   Thank You   Number
Card Sent   Sent   Received   Sent   Attending

Name

Address

Telephone Number

E-mail Address

Gift

Save The Day   Invitation   R.S.V.P   Thank You   Number
Card Sent   Sent   Received   Sent   Attending

Name

Address

Telephone Number

E-mail Address

Gift

Save The Day   Invitation   R.S.V.P   Thank You   Number
Card Sent   Sent   Received   Sent   Attending

Guest List Planner

Name

Address

Telephone Number

E-mail Address

Gift

| Save The Day Card Sent | Invitation Sent | R.S.V.P Received | Thank You Sent | Number Attending |

Name

Address

Telephone Number

E-mail Address

Gift

| Save The Day Card Sent | Invitation Sent | R.S.V.P Received | Thank You Sent | Number Attending |

Name

Address

Telephone Number

E-mail Address

Gift

| Save The Day Card Sent | Invitation Sent | R.S.V.P Received | Thank You Sent | Number Attending |

Name

Address

Telephone Number

E-mail Address

Gift

| Save The Day Card Sent | Invitation Sent | R.S.V.P Received | Thank You Sent | Number Attending |

Name

Address

Telephone Number

E-mail Address

Gift

| Save The Day Card Sent | Invitation Sent | R.S.V.P Received | Thank You Sent | Number Attending |

Made in the USA
Monee, IL
23 August 2021